SCOTLAND'S ECONOMY
Claiming the Future

VERSO

London · New York

In association with the Scottish Trades Union Congress

First edition published by the STUC, April 1989
Second edition published by Verso in association with the STUC, September 1989
© STUC and Verso

Verso
UK: 6 Meard Street, London W1V 3HR
USA: 29 West 35th Street, New York, NY 10001-2291

Verso is the imprint of New Left Books

ISBN 0—86091—984—6

Acknowledgements

Indispensable help in the conduct of research related to this work was provided by Christopher Madigan, Martin Gostwick, Charles Locke, Hugh Maguiness and Irene Sweeney.

Thanks are also due to Dennis Henry of PE Inbucon for access to survey material.

Typeset and printed in Great Britain by Hampden Advertising Ltd (TU), Glasgow G2 8QD

PREFACE

Two years ago the STUC published an economic strategy for Scotland. We called it *Scotland: A Land Fit for People*. As part of the extensive research which lay behind that document, we uncovered evidence of deeply disturbing changes in the ownership and control of the Scottish economy.

One year ago the STUC established a working group with a view to analysing these changes in ownership and control in more detail — and drawing policy implications from the analysis. This pamphlet is the result of a year's work by that working group. It is a discussion document, not a statement of STUC policy, and the views expressed are those of its authors. I believe, however, that it is one of the most penetrating pieces of policy analysis conducted for the trades union movement.

It provides a detailed analytic background to, and an economic policy for, our much needed Scottish Assembly. I am confident that *Scotland's Economy: Claiming the Future* will be of immeasurable help in winning a consensus on the issues facing the Scottish Assembly and the powers it needs to tackle them.

Campbell Christie
General Secretary
Scottish Trades Union Congress

1 INTRODUCTION

Scotland is at a crossroads, economically, socially and politically. A significant part of its industrial capacity has been lost. What remains is in danger. Many of its people are unemployed, and over the last ten years 150,000 Scots, if we include family members, have left to seek work elsewhere. It is the argument of this pamphlet that the people of Scotland have to take urgent steps to secure their economic future, and the following chapters will seek to develop some of the practical proposals made two years ago in the STUC's policy document, *Scotland: A Land Fit for People.*

We start with the dimensions of the crisis. Norway and Denmark both have populations of roughly the same size as Scotland. At the beginning of the century Scotland possessed a far more productive economy than either. Output per head was more than 50% higher. Now the position has been reversed. Scotland's GDP per head is only 89% that of Denmark and 76% of Norway's.

The problem is not just that Scotland's industrial workforce is today only 58% of what it was in 1972. It is that Scotland has become less productive and less competitive compared to other nations. This is where it is correct to speak of de-industrialisation. Even within Britain, compared to the south

Figure 1.1

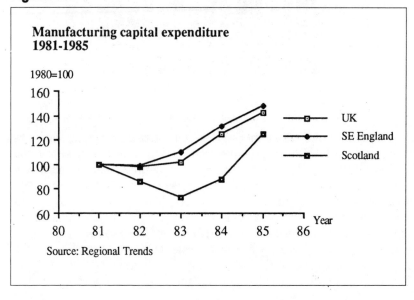

east of England, Scotland's proportion of manufacturing capital expenditure has fallen sharply in recent years. (Figure 1.1)

Government apologists have claimed that the fall in industrial employment itself is nothing to worry about: that it is happening everywhere else and that there is a secure future in services and high technology. (Figure 1.2) Unfortunately, however, the high technology industries are not generating greater levels of employment. They employ today no more than they did in the 1970s. More fundamentally, an expanding service sector cannot be sustained without manufacturing. Manufacturing itself creates the demand for many services, and what can be spent on housing, education and health will ultimately depend on the productivity and size of industry. The balance of payments crisis now facing Britain as a whole shows this only too clearly.

Figure 1.2

In addition to this loss of industry, there is further change in Scotland's economic life which will be explained here. It is the loss of economic control. Earlier this century the great bulk of industry was owned and controlled from Scotland and a significant part of it was also publicly and democratically accountable. Heavy engineering, coal, steel, chemicals, machine tools, textiles and printing provided the basis for a highly integrated national economy. A few islands of external control existed but only as islands.

Today the situation is reversed. It is the Scots-controlled firms which are the islands. Previously ecomonic linkages ran *within* Scotland between its firms and industries. Now they tend to run into and out of Scotland within individual firms. Managerial decision-making and research and development are largely concentrated outside Scotland, and the country has only half the British average of research and development personnel within its industrial workforce. This affects not just the integration of the Scottish economy, but, perhaps still more seriously, its ability to create and develop new products. For the country that pioneered the applications of science to industry, the consequences of this could hardly be more serious.

These two processes, de-industrialisation and the loss of economic control, will not be examined in this pamphlet simply as a matter of academic interest. It will be done in order to identify how the people of Scotland can reverse these trends and gain at least a measure of control over their economic destiny. It is this future which is to be claimed.

2 WHO OWNS? WHO CONTROLS?

At the beginning of the century

A hundred years ago virtually the whole Scottish economy was controlled and very largely owned from within Scotland. The shipbuilding industry, the biggest in the world, employed 60,000 people and was pioneering the use of steel and steam turbine engines.

Shipbuilding was closely integrated with the iron, steel and coal production and together they provided the commercial basis for a massive infrastructure of railways, canals and docks. Railway and locomotive construction provided another major sector of production and exporting. Scottish bridge builders and civil engineers were among the world leaders – producing structures such as the Forth Bridge and smaller replicas across the British empire. In chemicals, printing and to a lesser extent textiles and food production, Scottish firms had secured dominant positions in their respective markets.

Not all these firms were entirely owned from within Scotland. There was considerable share ownership in the railway companies from England. Some of the firms, or their owners, had themselves moved to Scotland: William Pearce, founder of Fairfields; Yarrows shipbuilding and, considerably earlier, some of the industrialists in cotton textiles. There was also a considerable level of interlinkage between Scottish and English firms (in, for instance, railways) and a very high level of reliance on empire markets. Nonetheless, virtually every firm was run from Scotland. The commercial and administrative head offices and the design departments were in Edinburgh, Glasgow or Dundee. They were serviced by a separate Scottish banking system which itself operated on a global scale directly exporting capital to the Americas and Australasia. At the level of the British state, Campbell Bannerman, Asquith, Bonar Law, members of the Scottish legal banking and commercial dynasties, held the office of prime minister almost continuously for the first two decades of the twentieth century.

A typical figure of this period was Sir Charles Tennant, Asquith's father in law, who controlled a large slab of the chemical and metal producing industries. His main company became a dominant part of United Alkali, the world's largest chemical firm, based in Liverpool, in 1885. He was a major owner of the Tharsis Sulphur and Copper company (originally French and operating in Spain) which supplied both the steel and chemical industries with key raw materials. He collaborated with the Swede Arthur Nobel to establish at Ardeer in Ayrshire the Nobel Explosives factory, which, together with counterpart firms in Germany and America, owned the world monopoly for dynamite production. Together Nobel Explosives and United Alkali eventually spawned ICI. Tennant also had interests in the Caledonian Railway, and Steel Company of Scotland, locomotive construction, coal, electricity generation and the Clydesdale Bank.

In Tennant we have the archetypical Scottish entrepreneur: locally based and operating within the indigenous financial system but facing out to England, the empire and the world, drawing capital and forming syndicates wherever the terms were best. Two dozen such families, the Colvilles, Lithgows, Weirs, Coats, Baxters, Stephens, controlled between them the great bulk of the Scottish economy.

The Scottish economy today

Today the picture is transformed. There are virtually no major firms that are fully owned and controlled from within Scotland. In a seminal article written in 1975 John Firn made this assessment:

"... it is no longer possible to assume that the majority of the important strategic decisions shaping the future course of development of the manufacturing sector in Scotland, and especially those made for the important high technology sectors such as electronics and chemicals, are made within Scotland or indeed are made with predominantly Scottish interests in mind ... the power of Scotland to shape or even strongly influence her own economic future has been, is being and probably will continue to be strongly eroded ... it is becoming increasingly difficult to talk meaningfully of a distinct 'Scottish economy' except in a strict geographical sense."[1]

This pessimistic forecast has proved accurate. The change in ownership in Scottish manufacturing over the past two decades is shown in Figure 2.1.

Already in 1968 less than half of Scottish manufacturing employment was in Scottish-owned firms. Within ten years this had been reduced to just over a third. Although the statistics are not as comprehensive as we would want (the fullest survey being that for 1977), the trend is clear. So also is the dominance of the external firms in terms of size. The average size of the Scottish-owned firms was less than one third that of the average British or American firm in 1973, 1977 and 1983. (Figure 2.2)

This concentration of Scottish ownership among the smaller firms coincides with what we know about the industrial distribution of external ownership. The survey for 1973, at the conclusion of the long post-war period of branch plant investment, shows that external firms tended to be concentrated in the industries which were growing fastest, such as electrical and instrument engineering, or which required high capital, high tech inputs, such as

---

1. John Firn, 'External Control and Regional Policy', in Gordon Brown ed., 'Red Paper on Scotland', EUSPB 1975.

Figure 2.1

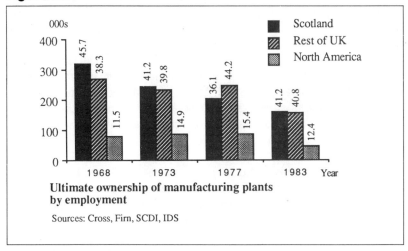

Ultimate ownership of manufacturing plants
by employment

Sources: Cross, Firn, SCDI, IDS

Figure 2.2

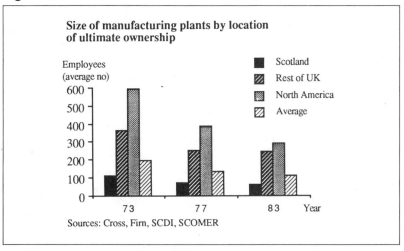

petroleum products and chemicals. Conversely, in sectors which were not growing quickly or with traditional technologies, Scottish ownership remained strong. The biggest of these were textiles and paper, printing and publishing. The large food, drink and tobacco sector, including the expanding and profitable whisky industry was about 50/50 — still a greater than average level of Scottish ownership. In shipbuilding there remained significant Scottish ownership — with much of the remainder in the public sector. (Figure 2.3)

Moving forward from 1973 and 1977 to 1983, the figure for surviving Scottish

Figure 2.3

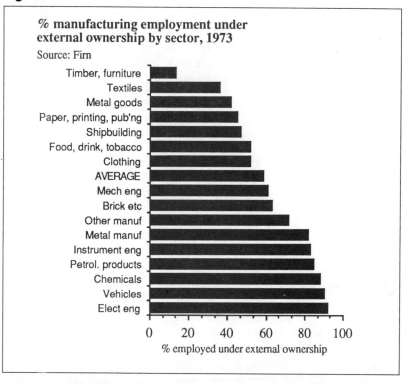

% manufacturing employment under external ownership by sector, 1973

Source: Firn

ownership might appear to give some ground for hope that the trend towards external ownership is coming to an end. The 41% Scottish ownership compares favourably with 36% in 1977. But this would be a misleading conclusion on two grounds. First, it was 41% of a much smaller total. There were 170,000 fewer manufacturing jobs in 1983 compared to 1977, and the higher percentage of surviving Scottish jobs simply indicates that externally-controlled branch plants proved to be more vulnerable during the massive world recession of the early 1980s. The surviving external firms were still much bigger than the surviving Scottish firms. The second reason why the 1983 figure does not give any ground for optimism is the date of the survey. The recession of 1980-4 was followed by a massive wave of external takeovers — often of a highly speculative kind.

The take-overs

In the two years 1985 and 1986, external takeovers cut the amount of capital controlled by Scottish-registered commercial and industrial companies from £4,672 million in 1985 to £2,278 by the beginning of 1987. This calculation is from the management consultants PE Inbucon. They also show that the firms taken over tended, quite predictably, to be the most efficient and profitable Scottish companies. Those taken over during these two years controlled 37% of the turnover but 49% of the profit income. The list of the principal takeovers, 1970 to 1987, speaks for itself and highlights the scale of the upturn which took place between 1984 and 1987.

Table 2.1 Major Scottish Companies taken over 1970—86

Name	Taken over by	Location	Year
Gourock Ropework	British Ropes	Rest of UK	1971
Wm Teacher	Allied-Lyons	Rest of UK	1976
Barr & Stroud	Pilkington	Rest of UK	1977
SUITS	Lonhro	Rest of UK	1979
Inveresk Paper	Georgia Pacific	N America	1982
Anderson Strathclyde	Charter Consolidated	South Africa	1983
Amalgamated Distilled Products	Argyll Group	Rest of UK	1984
F Miller (Textiles)	Vantona Viyella	Rest of UK	1984
Stenhouse	Reed Stenhouse	Rest of UK	1984
Arthur Bell	Guinness	Rest of UK	1985
House of Fraser	Al-Fayed Inv Trust	Egypt	1985
Brownlee	Meyer	Europe	1986
Coats Patons	Vantona Viyella	Rest of UK	1986
Distillers Company	Guinness	Rest of UK	1986
Don Brothers, Buist	Shell	Rest of UK	1986
Scottish Agricultural Industries	ICI	Rest of UK	1986
United Wire	Scapa Group	Rest of UK	1986
Yarrow	CAP Group	Rest of UK	1986

Sources: Inbucon, IDS, Scottish Business Insider, STUC

There has been no full analysis of the takeovers which have taken place since 1980. But for the fifteen years between 1965 and 1980 a comprehensive study has been made. The survey, by researchers at the Fraser of Allander Institute, covered 154 takeovers.(2) We will look later at their conclusions about the consequences of takeover. Immediately, however, our interest is in what the study has to tell us about where the takeovers were industrially concentrated. Table 2.2 indicates that this was principally those industries

---

2 B. Ashcroft and others 'The Economic Effects of Inward Acquisition of Scottish Manufacturing Companies 1965–1980', IDS 1987.

where Scots firms still held fairly dominant positions (paper, textiles and mechanical engineering) or in electronics where the few Scottish firms were also highly profitable and growing fast. It would appear that this pattern has been largely preserved — although on a much larger scale — since 1980.

Table 2.2 Industrial Breakdown of Takeovers 1965—1980

Industry 1968 SIC*	No of Companies	Employment in year of takeover	% total employed in industry 1972
Food, drink, tobacco	12	3058	3.20
Chemicals	2	—	—
Metal manufacture	4	1105	2.51
Mechanical engineering	9	6789	8.85
Instument/electrical eng	5	3683	5.28
Textiles	4	4374	6.13
Timber, furniture	4	985	4.14
Paper, printing, publishing	8	6582	13.30
Others	6	—	—
Total	54	31722	4.83

Source: IDS   *Standard Industrial Classification

What's left?

Somewhat surprisingly there are no accessible statistics on what proportion of employment or capital operating in Scotland is today controlled from within Scotland. However, the STUC data base on Scottish registered firms does at least give some indication of trends since the early 1980s. Taking the 140 largest of the Scottish-registered firms in 1979, Figure 2.4 shows the same firms in 1986 and divides them up, by turnover, in terms of those now 100% controlled from outside Scotland and those still formally controlled from within Scotland. From this we can see that about half of the biggest Scottish registered firms of 1979 were by 1986 externally controlled (although it should be noted that some of this external control already existed in 1979). This itself, however, is only part of the story. A large slab of those not 100% controlled by external companies were nonetheless effectively controlled from outside Scotland — including some of the biggest. Figure 2.5 shows the effect of shifting Burmah Oil, now entirely controlled by City of London institutions, from the Scottish to the non-Scottish category. A dozen other large Scottish-registered firms, the list headed by British Caledonian, could also quite justifiably be shifted. If this were done, the turnover represented by Scottish controlled firms would be reduced by a further third, even before the takeovers of 1987, 1988 and 1989.

Figure 2.4 (including Burmah Oil in Scottish registered companies)

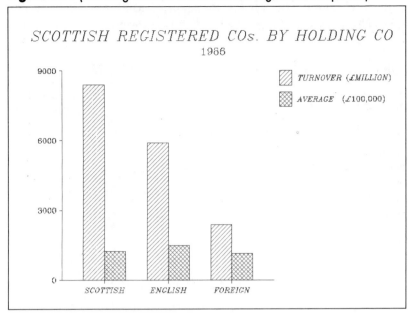

Figure 2.5 (excluding Burmah Oil from Scottish registered companies)

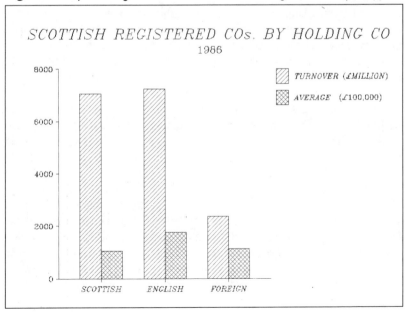

So, to sum up, we know, first, that a fifth of manufacturing employment is directly controlled from overseas. On this we have fairly accurate statistics. This foreign investment was mainly the result of the great wave of incoming branch plants which lasted from 1947 to 1973. The 20% figure has remained roughly the same since the 1970s — although the share of American ownership has fallen, even if still the biggest, and that from Europe and Japan increased. American-controlled jobs rose from just under 19,000 in 1950 to a peak of 86,000 in the early 1970s. At this point Scotland had the highest percentage of US investment per head outside Canada. From then on the number of American jobs fell back to 44,700 (about two-thirds of the total) in 1987. European countries, especially from within the EEC, accounted for 17,000 workers in 1987 (32% of overseas-controlled manufacturing employment). This was almost three times the proportion in 1960. Japanese investment, despite all the hopes, remains very small in terms of the numbers employed. In 1987 there were only ten plants employing a total of 1,500. (Figure 2.6)

Figure 2.6

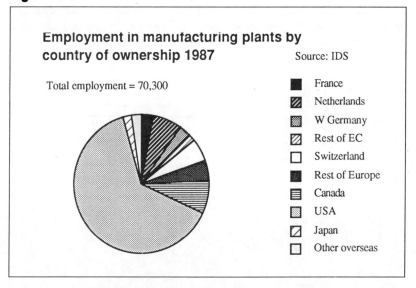

However, undoubtedly the biggest single area of external control remains that represented by British firms and conglomerates from the City of London. Taking into account wholly controlled Scottish-registered firms and those substantially controlled through dominant shareholders, such firms would seem to represent well over half of Scotland's manufacturing capital. There is unfortunately little doubt that the trend to takeover — at least of any remaining major Scottish firms — will continue. Collins and Scottish and

Newcastle are the most recently threatened, although S&N appears to have been rescued by the Monopolies Commission — at least for the time being. Morever, the privatisation of public sector industries and utilities has brought large additional slabs of resources on to the market and these have in general ended up under City of London control. In a sense, perhaps the change here may not be that great. The public sector was not Scottish, in terms of ownership of capital, and the location of headquarters, even before the process of privatisation began, was largely outside Scotland. But these industries were at least publicly accountable through a parliament in which Scottish interests were represented and to this extent responded to Scottish industrial and social needs. British Gas, British Steel and most notably the British National Oil Corporation all had substantial research and development departments in Scotland and in the latter case the head office as well. Privatisation has generally seen ultimate control — as in the case of Yarrows, Scott Lithgow, Britoil, ROF — quickly pass into the hands of City of London conglomerates.

1992 and the coming of the Single European Market is only too likely to complete the process. Hence, our opening contrast with the situation at the beginning of the century. The rest of this pamphlet is about why this transformation should have taken place over the past forty years, about what the economic consequences have been, and — most important of all — what can be done about it.

3 MONOPOLY AND CONCENTRATION

The latest figures for industrial concentration in Britain (which themselves do not take account of recent takeovers) show that the top 100 firms were responsible for 42% of total manufacturing output. (Figure 3.1) This represents a significant increase in concentration since 1963 when the top 100 only produced 27% of output. If we turn to ultimate control, then the real level of economic concentration today is still higher. Many of the top industrial firms are either owned by big conglomerate holding companies or are under the influence of consortia of merchant banks and financial institutions. In Scotland, as we have seen, most of our industrial production is controlled from outside the country by British or American companies.

Figure 3.1

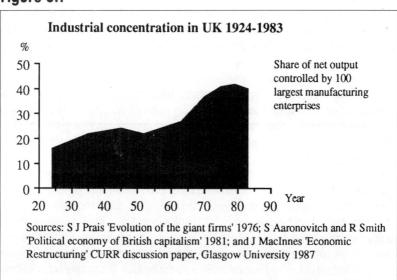

Industrial concentration in UK 1924-1983

%

Share of net output controlled by 100 largest manufacturing enterprises

Sources: S J Prais 'Evolution of the giant firms' 1976; S Aaronovitch and R Smith 'Political economy of British capitalism' 1981; and J MacInnes 'Economic Restructuring' CURR discussion paper, Glasgow University 1987

Why this trend to concentration and external ownership?

Wherever you travel in the western world and beyond, certain companies and their products provide familiar landmarks: Ford cars, Coca Cola drinks, Sony electrical equipment, American Express financial services, and a host of other operations.

Familiar though it may be today, such multinational business activity is a recent creation in historical terms. It was the British who started large-scale overseas investment in the 19th century. In 1855 Britain's overseas investments stood at £230 million. By the outbreak of the war in 1914, the total had grown to £4,000 million. Most of it, however, was not direct investment, and did not involve British firms actually building factories overseas. It was done by buying shares in overseas companies or lending money to foreign governments for the building of railways or docks. This portfolio (or indirect) investment was relatively short-term, and pursued the highest return without too much commitment to particular enterprises. British individuals and institutions funding the American railroads, for instance, did not seek to control the operation of the companies in which they invested.

Direct investment, in contrast, takes place when a company owned and controlled in one country establishes a production centre in another. Probably the first example of this in Scotland was the setting up of the Singer sewing machine factory on Clydeside in the 1860s. Such an investment is radically different from the portfolio type. First, the parent company exercises a degree of control over its foreign subsidiary. This may be quite minimal, as for example, the setting of profit targets. More typically the parent company will determine the nature of and level of the subsidiary's output, the technology employed and the markets in which products are to be sold. Following on from this is a second point. The subsidiary will not necessarily serve its domestic market in a direct way. It will often produce components for use *within* the internal economy of its international parent, and these will only be marketable as part of a composite product. Indeed today 40% of all world trade is of this kind. Within this international division of labour, the parent company invariably retains the strategic functions such as research, product development, design and marketing. Such global diversification has become increasingly the dominant trend since the last war.

Why, therefore, does this overseas investment take place? What impels companies to take the risk of moving their production into other countries? There are no uncontested answers to this question. One widely held view is that this type of overseas investment results from the way in which capitalist economies grow and develop. As the efficient size of production units increases, some firms become dominant within the domestic market, seek to remove effective competition and secure monopolistic profits. When this occurs across the economy as a whole, the opportunities for maintaining such monopolistic profits diminish and it becomes necessary to find investment opportunities overseas. This view directly links overseas expansion to monopoly and industrial concentration. Other economists, those who defend a free market viewpoint, contest this link. They argue that firms rank the profitability of various potential projects and that only those which promise a return greater than the expected rate of profit will be acceptable. In both cases, however, the implication is that there is a limit, in the short-run at least, to the profitable opportunities within the domestic economy. Faced with this problem, firms look for such opportunities in other countries.

The first phase of this type of direct investment from Britain was associated with companies involved in the overseas extraction and marketing of raw materials. Examples would be oil (British Petroleum, Burmah and Shell), natural fats (Unilever), non-ferrous metals (Rio Tinto Zinc), chemicals (ICI). This pattern was well established by the first world war. Increasingly, however, firms have developed overseas production in order to manufacture products originally produced in their own country. The motive here is principally that of penetrating foreign markets and securing cheaper labour. The establishment of British motor plants in South Africa would be an example. Another would be the establishment of American plants in Scotland in the three decades after the last war. The American companies imported more productive technology, and could both produce more efficiently and take advantage of cheaper labour. At the same time they were able to pay wages that were often higher than those of local producers and so secure the most skilled labour.

Possession of *trans*-national organisation also gives such firms a number of other advantages. In the same way that a dominant national firm can price its competitors out of the market, so a multinational firm will often have the ability to use its own internal 'transfer' prices to subsidise production for as long as it takes to remove the local competition. Once this has been done, it can behave as a monopoly producer, and then, in turn, use transfer pricing in the opposite direction. The company's export of components to its factories or depots elsewhere can be underpriced so that profits accumulate where taxes are lowest.

Are these giant firms national or international?

Are these companies therefore, fully international and genuinely free from any particular national control or responsibility? This is a quite difficult question. Over the past twenty years two processes have been at work. As the post-war boom came to an end, there has been intensified competition between these giant companies. Survival has largely depended on how much research and development could be invested in new products and how quickly firms could bring their production, on a world scale, into line with the cost-cutting opportunities offered by the new technologies. Consequently, because of the scale of investment needed, considerable importance has been attached to *joint* research programmes negotiated between major producers and also to reallocating particular stages of production to those locations where the appropriate labour, whether it be computer programmers or unskilled assemblers, is cheapest and most readily available. To this extent the operations of these firms have become *more* international. The capitalist world now has only three or four dominant aircraft producers and only four or five dominant producers in fifth generation computing.

At the same time the scale of the investment needed, and the character of the markets means that state support is crucial. In aircraft production and advanced computing, for instance, governments are major purchasers, and there are very few firms that are not 'national' in the sense of being principally owned and controlled through the financial institutions of a particular country. Even the exceptions, like Unilever, Royal Dutch Shell and Phillips, are seen as joint firms with a dual Anglo-Dutch or Dutch-American nationality. The patronage, protection and direct subsidies provided by governments for 'their' companies have played a key role in their ability to compete effectively on the world scene.

In this sense the giant firms are in almost all cases *national* rather than international. Many of America's biggest firms are heavily dependent for both research and for the biggest part of their domestic market on the US defence department. In engineering a third of all production goes to defence. The profits and technological advances secured in this area are crucial in maintaining the overall level of growth. In Japan there has been an even more elaborate system of state support. For the forty years since the last war a single ministry has been responsible for the strategic upgrading of technology, the importing and licensing of patents and the stage-by-stage build-up of an internationally competitive potential. The Japanese state first sponsored the production of high volume quality steel as the basis for moving into shipbuilding, motors and consumer durables. and then used this to open the way to electronics and computing. As part of this process the Japanese government actively sponsored subcontract 'partnership' relations between the big firms and their suppliers, and in this way enabled a relatively small permanent core workforce (highly-paid, highly trained and highly susceptible to control) to be maintained alongside a poorly-paid temporary workforce mainly employed in the subcontract firms.

Today Britain has only a small minority of the world's very big firms. Most of the biggest are American, Japanese or German. (Figure 3.2) Of the dozen or so British firms in the top hundred the majority are primarily involved in raw material extraction (especially oil, gas and metals). British firms have lagged behind in the race to innovate new technologies in capital equipment and consumer goods, and this is at least partly because of the relatively small size of the British economy. There are of course other very important factors. Recent government policies (ending controls on capital export, a high international valuation of the pound and high interest rates) have certainly penalised domestic investment. But this question of size is important. A small domestic market and a small volume of state purchasing, in international terms, means a smaller total volume of investment available for technological

Figure 3.2

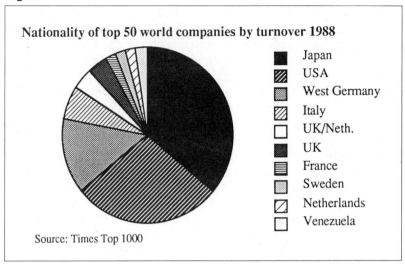

Nationality of top 50 world companies by turnover 1988

- ■ Japan
- ▨ USA
- ▨ West Germany
- ▨ Italy
- ☐ UK/Neth.
- ▨ UK
- ≣ France
- ▨ Sweden
- ▨ Netherlands
- ☐ Venezuela

Source: Times Top 1000

transformation. Britain, like other European Community countries, cannot match the volume of research and development in Japan or America. This is why big business within the European Community favours the creation of a single market and a single central purchasing agency for research and defence contracting. This, it is felt, will enable European-based firms to compete more effectively. However, this is unlikely to help any but the strongest British firms. Given the technological lead of French and especially German firms, and the fact that there can only be one or two major European producers, it is they that are likely to emerge in most sectors as the dominant producers.

Do branch plants help Scotland to remain technologically competitive?
This poses a basic question. If it is this type of global organisation, and large-scale state sponsorship, that is essential for technological competitiveness, isn't it inevitable that small countries like Scotland will have to accept that their economic future depends on the attraction of branch plants? What is more, does this not demand that the labour movement adopts a more 'business-friendly' attitude?

To get an answer to this we have to consider the recent technological developments a bit more fully.

There is fairly general agreement that the type of production processes pioneered by Japanese firms, and now widely copied by American and German firms, permit rapid increases in productivity. Big firms using these techniques have been able to grow at fairly unprecedented rates. Flexible manufacturing systems in particular make possible a far more intensive use of capital. Flow lines are speeded, the waste of both materials and time is cut, and workers themselves are involved in maintaining quality. The key personnel element is the creation of cell-based teams with interchangeable skills and a strong orientation towards cooperation with management in continually upgrading models and innovating new techniques.

Matched against this, however, are a number of special conditions. First as we noted, when discussing Japan, the stability of the core workforce, and in large measure its motivation for cooperation with management, depends on offloading risk and the impact of market fluctuations onto supply firms. Sourcing a large proportion of components outside the core factory, cutting inventory stocks and enforcing a just-in-time schedule on suppliers, buffers the core firm against the impact of market downturn. It does so, however, only by displacing the burden onto a tied, dependent layer of subcontractors. In certain circumstances this could seriously affect the resilience of an economy and in particular the formation of new firms. The second condition follows on. The inferior pay, conditions, employment level and training of the workers in the subcontract firms will also have a social cost. Unemployment, poverty, lack of training ultimately cost money. Moreover, a two-tier labour market of this kind will also make it much more difficult to develop effective trade union structures that are able to bargain on an industry-wide basis. So although the new techniques will permit greater levels of productivity and economic growth for the core firms, the weakness of the trade union movement may mean that, as in Japan, the new wealth will be less equitably distributed.

The third special condition concerns the *international* dimension of these new production techniques. It is this that largely supplies us with the answer to our original qeustion.

Globally, the various phases of production will be unevenly distributed. Part of the way in which productivity is geared up in the core firms is not just by off loading costs onto smaller companies but also onto smaller and weaker economies. Research, design and development will almost always be located where the firm's own government, Japanese or American, physically directs its research expenditure. It will not exist within most branch plants. The benefits of high productivity growth, in terms of technology development and innovation, will only reach branch plants second hand. An example would be Scotland's high-technology electronic firms. Almost all are externally-owned. Some perform relatively sophisticated functions and consume a large proportion of Scots trained technicians and graduates. But none conduct any form of fundamental research. In the last three years there have been virtually no Scottish industrial partners for European-funded research programmes in electronics.(1)

Within this international division of labour Scotland still has a relatively sophisticated industrial infrastructure. It is therefore able to attract those branch plants performing skilled processes that require ample supplies of well-trained skilled and scientific labour. But even these hi-tech plants demand sourcing at lower levels of skill and require the existence of subcontract firms which can draw on a large pool of part-time and temporary labour. We will look at some of the consequences in the next section. But in terms of off loading risk and social costs this has serious implications for the regional economy. The presence of branch plants will tie up a large area of productive capacity in low level subcontract production. The benefits from technology transfer will therefore be limited. The major short-term cost will be the unavailability of this capacity for all-round economic development. The longer-term cost will be the vulnerability of the economy to changes in the wider economic climate and to branch plant closure. Periodic corporate restructuring is more or less inevitable, and it will usually be the overseas branch plants that go first.

It is in this context that a structurally divided labour force, and a weakened trade union movement, could be so dangerous. The new character of corporate investment demands a more effectively organised trade union movement with active national and international links and a rapid communication of information. The Caterpillar episode showed this. If the labour movement is weakened rather than strengthened, the consequences will be far more severe than in the core 'parent' economies of America or Japan. There the systematic weakening of trade unions may simply mean a more unequal division of wealth. In countries like Scotland it would immediately weaken the fight to ensure that all workers have decent conditions and access to secure occupational progress. In the longer-run it could threaten the technological viability of the host economy and produce a dependence whereby whole areas of technology could be removed overnight without any redress. Accordingly, it can be reasonably argued that to base economic strategy purely on the attraction of branch plants, especially when bought at the expense of 'no unions' or business unionism, provides a very shaky foundation for real economic growth.

Why have so many of Scotland's own big firms been taken over in the last few years?

The final question to be raised regarding external control concerns the recent boom in takeovers. If it is a technologically dominant multinational firm which represents the leading edge of global productivity, why have so many of Scotland's own companies been gobbled up by outside firms over the past

---

1. Report in Glasgow Herald 14 November 1988; J. Henderson 'Semiconductors, Scotland and the International Division of Labour', Discussion Paper 28, CURR, Glasgow University 1987; R.A. De Mellow 'Trends in Employment in Industrial Research and Development in Scotland', Scottish Economic Bulletin, June 1988.

decade? Why, in particular, are City of London conglomerates willing to buy up large slabs of assets — in some cases industrial capacity being shed from the state sector?

In the 1970s there is some evidence to suggest that the effect of takeover, often in the form of industrial merger, was relatively benign. It would mean the loss of head office functions from Scotland. It consequently reduced the volume of business for the Scottish financial services sector in accounting, banking and law. But it often provided the capital required for re-equipment to sustain employment in companies that might otherwise have found it difficult to meet internationally competitive standards.

In the 1980s the scale of takeovers has been much bigger and their record has been considerably less defensible. Most have come from British firms — although some have been European or Australian. Many have had a strongly speculative element to them and have been launched by conglomerate companies specialising in buying up assets in quite diverse industries. Sometimes the motive has been to capture those areas of market strength in which Scottish firms have developed profitable brand names, Whisky, some areas of publishing, insurance might be good examples of this. These represent readily marketable assets. In other cases it may be to consolidate a firm's grip on a particular type of productive capacity. The takeover of firms in heavy industry, such as Babcock Power, would illustrate this. In other cases it is simply to strip assets and sell off a firm's share investments, its research base and particularly its property portfolio.

The ability of City of London-based firms to launch such takeovers was, as we noted in the last section, particularly marked in the mid-1980s. They were able to do so at least in part because of the wider strategy of the British government to develop London as a banking centre. The government's objective was to use the temporary windfall of the North Sea oil revenues to build up a raft of overseas investments that would sustain London as world financial centre into the 21st century. A necessary condition for this was a high international value for the pound, and generally high interest rates to sustain it. While this penalised long term industrial investment in Britain, it did attract large quantities of short-term money into London. It was this that fuelled the activities of those interested in takeovers with relatively short-term profit expectations and who, of course, had to finance money borrowed at very high rates of interest.

Some of the takeover battles of the last few years have achieved wide notoriety. One such was Guinness's capture of Scotland's largest drinks firm, Distillers. Most takeovers, however, occur with little publicity and these are far more typical. The purchase of Scottish interests by our case study company, Trafalgar House, took place, in the main, with little public fanfare, and in most cases resulted from sales of public sector assets. The examination of this

Figure 3.3

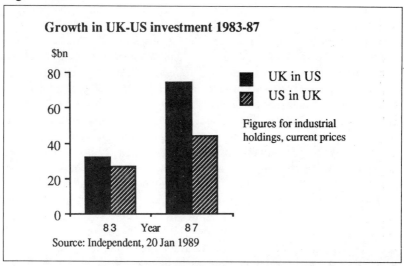

Growth in UK-US investment 1983-87

$bn

UK in US
US in UK

Figures for industrial
holdings, current prices

83   Year   87

Source: Independent, 20 Jan 1989

company also helps to illustrate some of the other points made earlier: the degree to which big business is dependent on direct state support; how far corporate planning takes place centrally and can give little or no consideration to the consequences for the local economy; and how far changes in state and company policy can have quite arbitrary and unpredictable effects. This is particularly significant in the case of Trafalgar House because of the degree to which it sought to enter and dominate a potentially strategic and dynamic sector of the Scottish economy: the oil construction industry.

Trafalgar House: a British conglomerate in Scotland

Trafalgar House is today the UK's 50th biggest quoted company with £1,500m capital. It started as a property and construction company, and developed very fast in the 1960s and 1970s, utilising funds from City of London institutions. In the 1970s and 1980s it sought to diversify its holdings into other sectors and now controls over 128 subsidiary companies. These are dispersed in four major areas: property and investment; construction and engineering; shipping, aviation and hotels; and oil and gas.

Trafalgar's presence in the Scottish economy arose mainly through the ownership of Redpath Dorman Long Limited in Cambuslang. This was acquired along with other UK steel fabrication businesses under the RDL name from the British Steel Corporation in 1982. The total cost was £10m. RGC Offshore of Methil was acquired from BSC in 1984 for £15m. This builds offshore oil platforms. Scott Lithgow on the Lower Clyde was acquired from British Shipbuilders in 1984 at what seems to have been a bargain basement price of £12m. This gave Trafalgar capacity for building warships, submarines and oil rigs. John Brown Engineering of Clydebank, which specialises in turbine production, was acquired in May 1986 as part of an £80m takeover of all the other businesses of the Sheffield-based John Brown. This included capacity for the production of tunnelling equipment and the manufacture of plastic and textile plants, oil and gas refineries, trailers and coach bodies.

These acquisitions were not random but, initially at least, part of a strategy to build up a preponderant position in the oil construction industry. Trafalagar House sought to place itself in a situation where it would be seen by British governments as the one firm capable of taking on competition from American and European firms in this field. This quickly placed Trafalgar at the heart of potentially the most dynamic sector of the Scottish economy.

At its height in 1985 the value of North Sea oil production reached £20,000m — compared with the total value of Scotland's non-oil GDP in the same year of £25,000m. The industry employed in all about 80,000 people, 5 per cent of the Scottish labour force, with the bulk of the expenditure being in constructing the infrastructure required for the extraction of the oil. This was the area which Trafalgar House sought to enter.

Up to 1985, at the time Trafalgar was acquiring its assets, 66% of the industry's activity was in the area of exploration and development and only 34% in production. Very quickly, however, the economic climate changed. The crude oil price fell from about $30 a barrel to a current average of around $15, and the proportion of construction and exploration work fell to 55%. So, although over the following three years oil production has remained at about 2.6m barrels a day, the labour-intensive work of developing new fields has contracted sharply, with the loss of something like 20,000 jobs.

In 1986 total UK equipment orders fell by 30%. The Kishorn (Wester Ross) platform builder Howard Doris, originally employing 3,000, called in the receiver. The remaining yards competed for what was left of the work. These were the American McDermott company's Ardersier yard with 1,000 employees, Highland Fabricators (owned by Wimpey, Brown and Root) at Nigg Bay, the French firm UIE at Clydebank and Trafalagar House with 2,700 workers at Scott Lithgow and 1,500 at RGC in Fife.

Corporate strategy and the state

Trafalgar House's objective at the beginning of the 1980s was to create a UK monopoly within the whole area of capital plant production. This included the building of refineries, oil rigs, chemical and textile plants, steelworks and turbines. This scale of activity would, it was hoped, enable the company to take on the big monopolies in the USA, Japan and Europe. In the oil rig sector its intention was to reach a size where it could very quickly match the American giants Bechtel and McDermott. It did so in the context of a stated commitment by the Thatcher government to support a British presence in offshore fabrication at this level. With this objective the company began a rapid process of acquisition in both Scotland and the North East of England. It merged its Scottish purchases with the Middlesborough fabrication yards of Redpath Offshore and Cleveland Offshore to form Trafalgar House Offshore Ltd. By the mid 1980s Trafalgar House had become the biggest steel fabricator in Europe.

None of this could have been achieved without very considerable goverment backing, and large quantities of public money. The company enjoyed very close relations with the Conservative Party, was the seventh biggest contributor to its funds in 1983, and had the Prime Minister's son on its payroll. The Prime Minister gave personal assistance in negotiating major overseas contracts such as the construction of the Sultan Qaboos University in Oman.

The speed of the company's growth in the field of steel fabrication was to a large extent the consequence of its ability to purchase capacity at very cheap prices direct from the public sector. This was the case with Redpath Dorman Long in 1981. It was even more the case with Scott Lithgow in 1984. The Glasgow Herald reported at the end of 1986 on the 'massive financial engineering which the group's balance sheet underwent before it was sold ... the net cost to the taxpayer of selling Scott Lithgow – put by ministers at the time at £71.4m – has soared way beyond that ... it has never been revealed that British Shipbuilders wrote off loans to Scott Lithgow of £240m before selling the yard. Half that total had only been lent to the Clyde subsidiary in the twelve months before the sale.'(2) In total a little short of £400m of public funds was put into Scott Lithgow to cover its debts and to make it an attractive purchase for Trafalgar House.

But neither this, nor other substantial state subventions, was able to provide a stable environment for the effective use of the massive steel fabrication resources now held by the company. The problem was not just the temporary decline in North Sea Oil business in 1986. There were also political difficulties. The close links with the British state, on which the company depended, proved to be highly vulnerable. In 1985 and 1986 the company suffered four major blows which were all blamed on the withdrawal of state support. The company lost out to Japanese competition on the contract for the second bridge across the Bosphoros – blamed by the company chairman on British government delays in agreeing a credit package. The Cabinet turned down the proposal by the Trafalgar House-led consortium, Euroroute, for a road and rail link across the Channel. The DTI rejected the Trafalgar House bid to buy the state-owned Vickers and Cammell Laird yards, VSEL, which build the Trident submarine. Shortly after this naval contracts, which the company had

2 Glasgow Herald, 1st December 1986.

previously been given reason to expect for its Greenock yard, were awarded to VSEL. In early 1986 the chairman of Trafalgar House, Sir Nigel Broackes, was publicly criticising the government and accusing it of losing direction. The reason for this breakdown in relations is not totally clear. It occurred in the aftermath of the Westland affair and in the run up the 1987 election when the government was faced with backbench revolts and a number of Cabinet resignations. The basic issue seems to have been serious strategic conflict within the City of London about which international trading bloc should have Britain's first loyalty, America or the EEC.

Whatever the reasons, the consequences for the company's ambitions in the oilrig and steel fabrication area were serious, and led to a significant reappraisal of strategy. The original decision to enter the field was, according to the company's chief executive, Eric Parker, to prevent the company's 'overexposure' to property. 'We therefore needed a fourth leg. We opted for oil and gas'. By July 1987 the company was selling off certain of its oil operations, Candecca Resources and Cambrian Exploration, to BP which the managing director of the company's Oil and Gas division explained thus: 'We are in a dealing world and we are simple shuffling the pack.'

As will have become clear, none of these business decisions were taken with any thought as to the strategic development of Scotland's economy. The point of reference was where Trafalgar House could best direct its investments within a massive array of subsidiaries operating across the world. In all these decisions state support was, negatively or positively, crucial. The scale of operations made this inevitable. But given the nature of relations between the state and different monopoly groups there was little or no space for coherence or direction. Effective economic planning, and the survival of Scotland's precious concentrations of engineering skills, went by the board. Scott Lithgow is mothballed. The Cambuslang plant has less than 400 workers left and the Methil yard has suffered heavy redundancies. For Trafalgar House as a company these concerns are of relatively small significance. At best they never constituted more than two percent of the company's assets. The Scott Lithgow site, four miles of prime river front land, may yet yield a handsome future dividend in property development. But the company itself has moved on. Other areas of super profit are opening up. As Sir Nigel Broackes put it in his 1988 annual report, 'development progresses on a scale hardly seen before this century and undreamt of until very recently.'

4 CONSEQUENCES FOR THE SCOTTISH ECONOMY

The previous two chapters have sought to examine the wider environment within which the Scottish economy operates. They have shown the degree to which Scotland's economic resources have passed into external control — and that this control now extends beyond manufacturing to the service sector, transport banking, tourism and distribution. The examples will also have made it clear that although this growth in external control has generally been exercised through privately-owned conglomerate companies, these companies are themselves highly dependent on backing from their own state (whether British, American or Japanese). This unpredictable mixture of big business investment and state support has provided a less than stable base for regional growth. This chapter will look in more detail at some of the consequences.

Although these have been investigated fairly widely over recent years, there is still plenty of disagreement over the relative merits of pursuing a growth strategy based on non-indigenous and externally-controlled companies. A useful guide to the debate and the evidence, at least for the period up to 1980, is provided by the study, referred to earlier, conducted by a team of Strathclyde University economists and funded by the Industry Department for Scotland, *The Economic Effects of the Inward Acquisition of Scottish Manufacturing Companies 1965–1980*. This catalogues a number of different ways in which external investment might have affected Scotland's economic and social development and attempts to match opposing views against the record for these years.

First, has external investment created more permanent jobs?

One argument against inward investment is that externally controlled plants are more likely to introduce capital-intensive technology — and hence employ less — and that they are also more vulnerable to closure. The argument in favour of investment is that without the introduction of internationally competitive, high profit and high investment technologies there would be little future for the Scots economy. The evidence, at least up to the early 1980s, does not indicate the branch plants were any *more* likely to close. If anything the indigenous plants were slightly more vulnerable. The numbers employed in *overseas*-owned branch plants (there are no figures for City of London controlled plants) fell from 110,000 to 72,000 between 1975 and 1985. But proportionately the fall in domestic manufacturing industry seems to have been even greater. By this token it has to be acknowledged that neither types

Figure 4.1

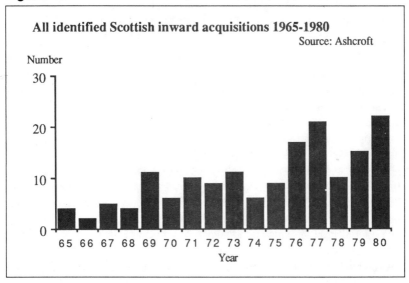

All identified Scottish inward acquisitions 1965-1980

Source: Ashcroft

Figure 4.2

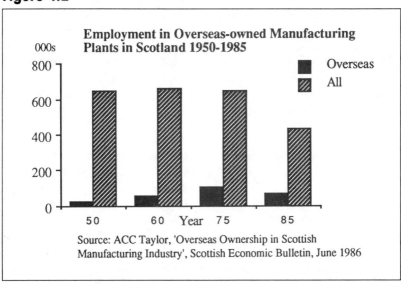

Employment in Overseas-owned Manufacturing Plants in Scotland 1950-1985

Overseas

All

Source: ACC Taylor, 'Overseas Ownership in Scottish Manufacturing Industry', Scottish Economic Bulletin, June 1986

performed particularly well. It is also clear that, as far as branch plants are concerned, they are best at creating jobs immediately on their establishment, but poor at maintaining *continued* job creation once their initial maximum is reached. (Figure 4.2)

This balance of achievement and failure is well illustrated by the electronics industry — in many ways the strongest advertisement for the benefits of inward investment. Even during the recession of the early 1980s the industry managed to increase its total turnover and sharply increase its share of Scottish industrial production to just over 10%. But actual employment has remained static at approximately 45,000 for the past decade. Compared to the growth industries of the past, shipbuilding or the consumer durables of the 1950s, electronics does not give any indication that it is going to be able to solve Scotland's unemployment problems.

Second, what kind of jobs are created?

Here the argument against external control is two-fold. First, the incoming branch plants have tended to replace engineering skills, involving apprenticeship and at least a limited career progression, with semi-skilled and part-time workers engaged largely in routine assemblage. Second, the more recent wave of inward acquisition has seriously weakened the pool of Scottish managerial and scientific personnel by removing headquarters staff and research departments to England or further afield. The most talented staff move up the company structure and out of Scotland. However, the counter argument makes the obvious point that without external investment these skills would have gone anyway, and the incoming investment brings with it not just higher technology but a demand for matching skills.

There can be no doubt that the most striking change in the character of employment opportunities over the past fifteen years has been the increase in part-time female employment. In 1972 there were 235,000 part-time women workers in Scotland. By 1988 the number had risen to 389,000 — 44% of *all* women working. This now represents 21% of the total labour force as against 11% in 1972. Many of these part-time workers have of course been employed in the expanding service sector. But to some extent the number of such part-time workers does reflect the changes in industrial structure. (Figure 4.3)

Again the electronics industry provides the most effective test. Of all industries it is the most dominated by external ownership (83% non-Scottish) and has the most advanced technology. The semiconductor industry, which makes up about a quarter of its turnover, is entirely owned by non-Scots companies. This sector employs a very high proportion of graduates (25% of their total labour force) and at the same time a large proportion of female and part-time shift workers in assemblage. The employment of graduates reflects the sophistication of the technology. Even here, however, the employment is of a routine and almost technician character. None of the firms has any significant facilities for basic research in Scotland, and the graduates — whose wages are half the level of their counterparts in the USA — are mainly used for testing and quality assurance.

Figure 4.3

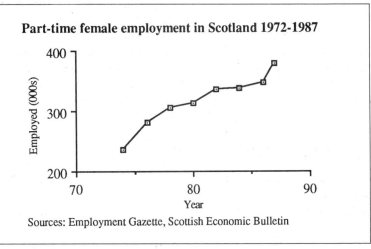

Part-time female employment in Scotland 1972-1987

Sources: Employment Gazette, Scottish Economic Bulletin

Does external investment lead to product innovation?

Product innovation is one of the most obvious benefits to be derived from incoming firms. New plants will produce new products. It cannot be disputed that external capital has often, particularly in the 1950s and 60s, introduced new product lines, and that these enabled existing Scottish firms to develop new components and enhance their own products. Yet at the same time there is always an element of risk. The new products may displace existing, less attractive Scottish products without providing any guarantee that the incoming multinational will continue to produce in Scotland once it has secured the market. Even with the best intentions, the pressures of a general recession, as in the early 1980s, can cause multinationals to rationalise and shift production lines elsewhere. The limited product lines remaining at the Singer plant at Clydebank in the 1970s are one example of how previous product rationalisation reduced the scope for effective competition with rival plants within the parent company — and made it very difficult for the plant's management to consider continuing independent production at Clydebank. More recently another and perhaps more serious danger has emerged. Incoming capital in the 1980s has tended to takeover existing firms, rather than set up new plants, and one major objective is that of securing the market assets represented by particular brand names. Once acquired the manufacture of these products can easily be removed elsewhere.

Another aspect of product innovation is of course technological progress in the way goods are produced. A plant within a world-level multinational will have access to best practice technology which provides the opportunity for a general diffusion within the rest of the economy. The use of new technology in retailing, banking and electronics has undoubtedly been advanced by the spread into Scotland of English-based superstores, international finance companies and US and Japanese semiconductor manufacturers. But how far is this new technololgy actually passed on? There is, for instance, no indigenous semi-conductor industry in Scotland today despite almost two decades of overseas controlled production, and even in the electronics industry as a whole there is a poor record of new firm foundation. In engineering Caterpillar innovated very sophisticated systems of automated production. But these were not accessible to local suppliers or engineering companies and were quickly removed overseas when the plant was closed

There is indeed a real danger of the opposite process taking place. Parallel to the acquisition and removal of brand name production, some companies will buy up indigenous firms in order to gain access to their research and development resources, patents and skilled and professional labour. In the biotechnology and health care sectors, for instance, it has been argued that the lack of a strong indigenous industry has led to Scottish R&D companies becoming mere suppliers of contract research to external firms with little benefit to the Scottish economy itself. The loss of Scottish regional influence within the nationalised industries, in coal and steel in particular, has been reflected in the run-down and ultimate removal of research laboratories which had historically played a major role in product and production innovation in supplier and consumer industries.

Indeed, recent government decision-making on research and development allocation in, for instance, military procurement, the Atomic Energy Authority, the National Engineering Laboratory and higher education mirrors this anti-regional bias. There is every indication that government policy is based on the assumption that production in regions like Scotland will be derivative and not involve basic research. A study conducted in the mid-1980s indicated that military contracts went disproportionately to regions that already had greater GDP per head and strongly increased differentials in favour of the south east.(1) Over the last two years regional policy and, more recently, training policy have been transformed. The old emphasis on uniform provision has gone. Instead grants and training are increasingly tied to 'local needs'. Smaller firms now get development grants to the extent they develop partnership relations with bigger firms.(2) Training is to be linked to *local* employer requirements. While on the surface this may sound unobjectionable, its consquence will be to reinforce, rather than overcome, existing regional

---

1 R. Fleming and P. Smith, 'An Enquiry into Defence Employment in Scotland', TURU (S) 1987; Professor Brian Robson's paper to the Social Research Association reported in The Guardian, 21 December 1987.

2 A. Young, Glasgow Herald, 8 January 1988; Independent, 9 January 1988

differences. Low skilled areas will remain in that position. Small firms will be tied to the local branch plants of externally-controlled big business. A hierarchy of regions will be consolidated — some with markedly inferior services and infrastructures — which will reflect the differing levels of types of production.

Has external investment created the basis for 'growth centres'?

However, it could be argued that, even though the level of production may not itself involve high level local research, it does at least provide the basis for new centres of production growth. Local firms have an opportunity to produce components. Their increasing skill and specialisation in a particular area will encourage further inward investment and a process of cumulative growth will begin.

Once more the electronics industry provides us with a test case. Its output has grown much faster that any other sector apart from oil and as fast as past 'growth centre' industries such as shipbuilding. Yet the record is poor. Only 10% of sourcing for semi-conductor production is Scottish. In electronics as a whole it is only 15%.(3) These disappointing figures would seem to derive not so much from bad local management as the actual character of modern multi-plant companies. Earlier this century locally-owned shipyards created a chain of linkages by which they were supplied a mass of often very sophisticated components. These made up well over half the value of a ship.(4) Today multinational companies develop their own internal specialisations on a world scale, and as we saw earlier tend to trade in-house. Recent trends to Japanese-style just-in-time-systems may do something to rectify this, but certainly give little indication of developing the type of technologically balanced relations that existed, for instance, between a shipbuilder and a turbine manufacturer.

Moreover, the tendency to supply a company's needs in-house applies not just to components but also to financial and business services. One of the strongest negative findings of the Strathclyde University study was the effect of external control on the banking and legal sector. Once a Scottish company has been taken over, it will be serviced legally and financially from its head office, and the specialist Scottish law and accountancy firms, banks and financial advisers dispensed with. This in turn reduces the pool of managerial advice and talent which in the past appears to have played an important part in sustaining the dynamic of new firm foundation.(5)

---

3 James McCalman 'What's Wrong with Scottish Firms? Local Sourcing in Scottish Electronics', Scottish Economic Bulletin, December 1985.
4 Report by the Shipbuilding Working Group, 'Strathclyde Built in the 1990s', Strathclyde Regional Council, May 1987.
5 Michael Cross, 'New Firm Foundation and Regional Development', Gower 1981.

Figure 4.4

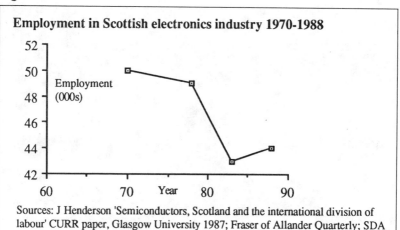

Employment in Scottish electronics industry 1970-1988

Employment (000s)

Sources: J Henderson 'Semiconductors, Scotland and the international division of labour' CURR paper, Glasgow University 1987; Fraser of Allander Quarterly; SDA

An interim balance sheet

What, then, are our conclusions? To the extent that City of London and overseas-controlled companies sustain well over a half of Scots industrial employment, it is unarguably the case that the country's productive capacity would today be massively lower without it. Some of the firms that have been taken over might have survived. Some new product lines might have been developed locally. But the infusion of capital and technology which has occurred since the last war clearly brought jobs where otherwise they would not have existed.

But this is not really the question. The problem is that Scotland's productive capacity is still proportionately much lower, compared to other countries, than it was a generation ago. Looking across to Norway, Denmark or the GDR, the country has regressed economically and not grown. The issue is therefore why this has happened and what forms of economic policy will make it possible to catch up in the future. (Figure 4.5)

The drawbacks of a reliance on external investment were, as we have seen, that it is on the terms set by firms which are managed elsewhere. Their policies do not, and could not, take into account the interests of the host economy itself. They invest capital. But they also ultimately must repatriate the profit. The surplus does not remain in the local economy. Their Scottish branches lack the independence or resources to enter effectively into local planning strategies. Compared with Italy, where there is a massively greater proportion of small and medium firms, or America, where its big cities still possess local banking systems, the massive urban conglomeration of West Central Scotland provides a very poor base for economic strategies based on

Figure 4.5

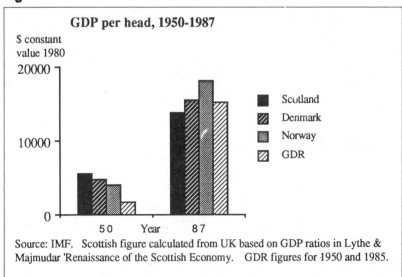

GDP per head, 1950-1987

$ constant value 1980

Scotland
Denmark
Norway
GDR

Source: IMF. Scottish figure calculated from UK based on GDP ratios in Lythe & Majmudar 'Renaissance of the Scottish Economy.   GDR figures for 1950 and 1985.

harnessing and directing local businesses.

What is even worse, the structure of the Scottish economy is far more fragmented than it was a generation ago. The linkages that could sustain spontaneous growth have one by one been broken, and recent research suggests that Scotland's economy today is *less* diversified than it was in the 1950s or 1930s. The new firms do not have the dense network of roots spreading through the rest of the economy which characterised the indigenous Scottish industries in capital goods and heavy industry. On this score, the policies of the 1960s and 70s which backed the sunrise industries 'against' coal, steel and shipbuilding have a good deal to answer for. However, before going on to examine what can be done now, we will look at one final case study: the lessons of the Caterpillar closure.

The lessons of the Caterpillar closure

The US-owned Caterpillar Company's plant at Uddingston was housed in one of the largest single-building factories in Europe. It employed over 1,000 men and women in 1986 and was one of the last major centres of the engineering industry in North Lanarkshire. Worldwide the twenty six Caterpillar plants had long dominated the world's construction equipment market, and still produced over a third of all heavy earth-moving tracked vehicles. Today the Uddingston factory is an empty shell. The workers and their prospects for a secure future have been discarded like so much rubbish. Yet only a matter of weeks before the bombshell of the closure announcement in Janaury 1987, the Caterpillar management at Uddingston had promised its workforce secure employment 'into the 1990s and beyond'.

The Caterpillar episode vividly illustrates some of the pitfalls of branch plant investment, and shows in particular that if power lies elsewhere, technological excellence and worker cooperation will be of very little value. By 1986 the Caterpillar factory was at the leading edge of technological advance. In the face of Japanese competition from Komatsu, the Caterpillar company had, as part of its global survival plan, already reorganised the factory using flexible manufacturing systems. Japanese-style supply procedures had been negotiated with subcontractors. Some of the most advanced automated manufacturing equipment in the world was installed during the six months before the closure announcement. In all this the workforced had cooperated fully, and the plant was known to be among the company's most efficient in Europe. But it did not do the slightest good. The decision to close was taken in the company's head office in America, and had, it seems, nothing to do with Scotland. It stemmed from pressures from stockholders for further worldwide capital rationalisation, maybe aided by fluctuations in the value of the dollar and the possibility of opening new factories in China. In the corporate-speak of Caterpillar's executives, Uddingston was the 'victim of the remedy'.

The unexpected and unexplained character of the decision, heard of first through news broadcasts, only added to the anger of the workforce. Within 24 hours they had occupied the plant. They were determined not to be passive victims and to take action that would directly assert their basic rights as workers to continued employment. Their immediate demand was that the Scottish Office act to compel the Caterpillar company to maintain the plant, and, if that failed, to back independent production on the site. To demonstrate their technical proficiency, and the need for what they produced, the occupying workers assembled, in record time, a tractor, the Pink Panther, which they then donated to Nicaragua. But despite very effective propaganda and a scale of support within the plant which initially brought junior and some middle management into the occupation, the occupation was ended after 103 days without any commitments about future employment.

Throughout the negotiations the company stuck to its initial position. Production of tractors and earth-moving equipment at Uddingston must stop. The factory might be used for some other purpose, but all the existing equipment had to be removed. Caterpillar did not want yet another producer in the same field. The main output from the Uddingston factory was components for tractor assembly and, as two-thirds of the plant's business, track spares. This large and expanding market was henceforth to be served from outside Britain. Detailed proposals were made to the company for maintaining spares production at Uddingston. The Local Government and

STUC initiated Working Party saw this as the most feasible way of keeping the plant open. The senior management at the plant also, privately, proposed a management buy-out on very similar lines. The company was implacably opposed. They intended to keep this market for themselves, and they did.

Why did the workers fail to keep the factory open — despite three months courageous and difficult struggle? It was not for want of public support. Something like £20,000 was donated each week by workplaces and through street collections. Nor was it for lack of determination on the part of the workers who defied a range of daunting challenges including court action. There were, however, three crucial areas of weakness — all to some extent related to the branch plant economy.

First, the workforce itself had been deprived of the full range of production and marketing skills. This made it much more difficult for the workforce, including the senior management, to plan alternative marketing or develop alternative products. The output of the Uddingston plant, despite its size, was marketed through the Caterpillar company and much of it traded to other factories. The factory lacked a sales department and had no research and development.

Second, the company was immensely powerful and could ultimately rely on the political backing of both its own government and of the political structures in Britain and Europe. The Conservative government lacked the political will, even if it wanted to use it, to attack the right of capital to go where it pleased. The British government could have threatened Caterpillar with exclusion from the British market. It could have set the Uddingston workers up in opposition. Other governments have done this. The Scottish Office did nothing. The EEC was no more helpful, and would certainly have ruled against any actions of the type just mentioned. Despite some initial expectations that Common Market provision must give workers some rights to employment, it was soon found that EC regulations are designed to protect the freedom of the market and that alone. In terms of investment the EEC regulations simply forbid governments to take any steps which might give 'its' investment unfair advantages. Nothing could have suited Caterpillar better.

Third, the organised trade union movement was unable to effectively counterbalance these hostile forces. Action was taken on many fronts, but it was not enough. There were significant technical weaknesses: a lack of information on how Caterpillar organised its supplies locally, and delays in establishing contacts with other Caterpillar workers elsewhere in Europe and America. There were also political weaknesses. In particular, the movement had not fully thought through how it could mobilise a response that was industrially effective in the new environment of the 1980s, and some sections of the movement believed that corporate restructuring had, eventually, to be accepted and future jobs depended on maintaining a "business friendly" image with external capital. This put serious limits on the fightback, and contributed to the loss to Scotland of both a factory and an entire sector of the industry.

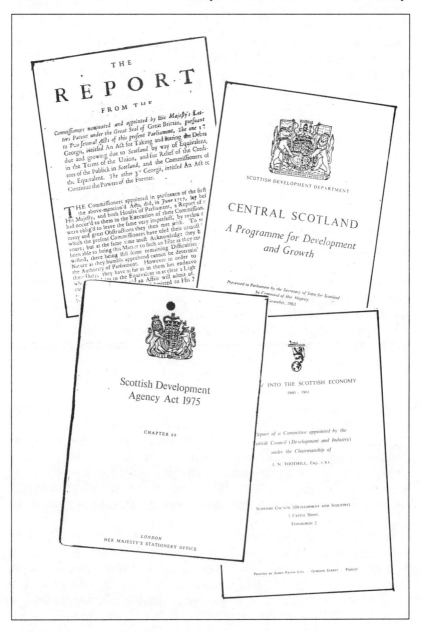

5 WHAT CAN BE DONE?

Can anything be done? In a period when many people are saying that the economy is best left to itself, it is important to start by reminding ourselves that the shape of the present-day Scottish economy resulted, for good or ill, very largely from a whole series of interventions by government.

As far back as the 18th century the Scottish linen industry and the herring fishing industry were actively promoted, and initially subsidised, by government boards set up under the Act of Union. The growth of shipbuilding and heavy industry in the 1890s and 1900s was largely sustained by government naval orders, and this government-direction of munitions production to Scotland was taken even further during the first world war and again in the late 1930s and 1940s. In the 1920s and 1930s the concentration of Scottish steel, coal and shipbuilding production into a cartel made up of a handful of firms was also sponsored, and partly subsidised, by the state. So also was the first establishment of industrial estates such as Hillington.

Since the last war almost every major development has been strongly influenced by government policy. At the end of the war the new political commitment to full employment was associated with an attempt to redistribute the location of industry towards areas, like the West of Scotland, where unemployment remained particularly high. Restrictions were placed on the expansion of factories across the south of England and grants given for relocation in what were called development areas. This resulted, as we saw in the second chapter, in the establishment of something like 200 branch factories. Many were from the south but a large number were direct investments by American companies who wanted a politically stable location within Europe. At one point in the 1950s 40% of all US direct investment in Europe was situated in Scotland. At the same time the hopes of wartime Scottish industrial planners for a far more comprehensive programme of industrial development were disappointed. The proposals in the Clyde Valley Plan of 1946 for linkages between a whole series of state and private industries never came to fruition. All that remains today of that post-war vision is the necklace of New Towns across Central Scotland.

To this extent it was the needs of the incoming branch plants that drove industrial policy in Scotland during the three decades after 1946. It was this that led to the creation, after a very long campaign in which the STUC played a leading part, of the strip mill at Ravenscraig. It also brought a thorough modernisation of Scotland's infrastructure. In 1960 the Toothill Committee, chaired by the Scottish manager of one of the biggest of the incoming companies, Ferranti, called for the transformation of transport systems, education, management training and the urban environment. The White Papers on the Scottish economic development of the 1963 and 1966 created new Scottish Office departments to ensure implementation, and very considerable funds were allocated to Scotland under the regional policies of both Conservative and Labour governments.

The benefits of these policies included the creation of over 100,000 new industrial jobs, most of them relatively skilled and well-paid, and the introduction of new technologies, particularly in the field of consumer durables. The weakness was the lack of comprehensive planning, the abandonment of the older indigenous industries — shipbuilding and heavy industry in particular — and hence the failure to integrate old and new and to root the new technologies in locally-controlled production. The branch plants remained, by and large, stand-alone. They utilised, and needed, the new social and industrial infrastructure. But they did not develop integral local links. When global recession hit their parent companies in the 1970s something like 30,000 of the new jobs were wiped out overnight. Moreover, because of the less than benign neglect of indigenous industry remaining local firms proved even more vulnerable. It was only at the very end of this period that the lessons began to be learnt and, as a result of pressure from the labour movement, initiatives made in the direction of comprehensive planning. Unfortunately, both the Scottish Development Agency and the British National Oil Corporation fell victim to the incoming Conservative government and were quickly transformed into quite different organisations. The record since th n has indeed been an appalling one. A string of key industrial installations disappeared within four or five years. These represented the result of years of planning and development, and included the giant car plant at Linwood, the British Aluminium smelter at Invergordon, the Fort William pulp mill, the cold strip mill at Gartcosh, the tractor and truck plant at Bathgate, the Carron Iron Works, the Springburn rail workshops, the coalmines supplying coking coal to Ravenscraig and the Clydebridge plate mill. In all 192,000 manufacturing jobs were destroyed in the first half of the 1980s.

The record of achievement

It would, however, be a mistake to dismiss the achievements of those three post-war decades. Government planning did stabilise significant new areas of employment. Still more important probably was the expansion of the public sector. The nationalised coal, steel, electricity and gas industries transformed Scotland's industrial infrastructure and provided cheap, reliable sources of energy and basic materials This was of crucial importance for the development of the private sector. The modernisation of coal production, electricity, railways, gas and later steel also provided a major stimulus for Scottish industries which produced capital equipment. Those major plants which survived as technological leaders into the 1970s and 80s largely did so on the basis of the technological challenges and markets which derived from publicly-owned industries: power production (Babcocks, Howden), telecommunications (Ferranti, Plessey), and coalmining (Anderson Strathclyde). Without this massive public sector, approximating to over a third of Scottish GDP in the 1970s, Scotland's economic plight would have been infinitely worse. It is indeed ironic that those who today talk about the superiority of the market over planning are the very ones who, at the same time as destroying the gains of past state intervention, have presided over the biggest ever decline in Scotland's private manufacturing base.

This, then, brings us back to the question of what can be done. How far is it possible, in face of the global power of big business, to take political action by which Scotland can achieve full and balanced economic and social growth?

The purpose of this pamphlet is not to add to the general lament. Nor is it to retreat into empty slogans. Least of all is it to throw up our hands and surrender to what sometimes seem to be omnipotent and inexorable forces. The history of the last ten years teaches us that this spells disaster for the Scottish people. We require, rather, a strategy which is based upon the realities of the world in which we live.

Issues for the Scottish people

In addressing such a strategy the four key issues which have to be confronted are:

1. Does the call for comprehensive, integrated planning — with cumulative linkages between industries — not assume a *closed* economy that will ultimately limit growth?
2. Is it possible to plan for an economy as small as Scotland's?
3. What leverage can be applied to those who currently control the bulk of Scotland's industrial resources — multinational companies and conglomerates mainly controlled from the City of London?
4. How are changes in the world economy likely to affect Scotland over the next few years, and in particular the emergence of a far more tightly-structured and aggressive trading bloc in Western Europe?

However, before going on to answer these questions, it is necessary to state one central assumption. None of these challenges can be met *without* a Scottish Parliament. Its creation is now crucial. Without it the Scottish people will not be able to tackle the obstacles that face them. We will also seek to show why, in answering each one of these questions, this Scottish Parliament must have power to raise taxes and to legislate on economic and social issues.

Integrated planning and the closed economy

Scotland's economic problem today is one of profound structural dislocation. The origins of this dislocation arose historically. It initially stemmed from the country's economic dependence on providing the capital equipment for Britain's empire. Scotland built the ships, the harbours, bridges and railways. With the collapse of this old type of colonial empire came a decline in the central components of the Scottish economy.

As we have seen, this basic economic dislocation has become far worse over the past decade and a half. It would be wrong to claim that, in terms of government policy, it has resulted simply from the unfettering of free market forces — because the old type of unfettered, fully competitive market hardly exists today. There is either little competition or massively unequal competition between corporate giants and small business minnows. It would also be wrong to say there is no planning. The big corporations which operate in Britain plan strategically on a world scale, depend on very high levels of inter-plant coordination, and are crucially reliant on support from their 'own' home state for credit, orders, research and development and often for simple, old-fashioned trade protection.

Scotland's problems, therefore, have worsened not because there has been no planning, no state intervention, but because it has been the wrong type of planning. Government policy, nothing else, has created conditions in which the giant City of London conglomerates have had the freedom to redirect economic resources in Scotland in ways which match their needs — and which have little or nothing to do with any form of comprehensive regional development. It is important to make these points because right-wing commentators have sought to protect the privileges of this kind of backstairs, democratically-unaccountable planning by denying that it is possible to plan at all.

There are certainly a number of different models of planning: central planning on a socialist basis; variants of central planning with elements of producer competition; indicative planning that uses profit incentives to coordinate public and private goals. Each have demonstrated their strengths and weaknesses over the past generation. But, in terms of performance, the biggest contrast is between the market economies which have given priority to a *planned* enhancement of industrial productivity in their home base and those which have not. The two countries with the lowest rates of growth, US and UK, are those which have instead given priority to enabling 'their' conglomerates and banking houses to maximise holdings where they are temporarily at least most profitable: overseas. In Britain the hallmark of the last ten years has been the giddy rise of overseas portfolio and short-term asset acquisition to a point where it exceeds domestic manufacturing investment. (Figure 5.1)

Figure 5.1

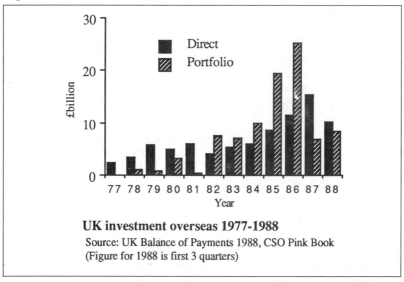

UK investment overseas 1977-1988

Source: UK Balance of Payments 1988, CSO Pink Book
(Figure for 1988 is first 3 quarters)

In contrast, the high-growth economies are those where the state places quite definite requirements on industrial producers. (Figure 5.2) We have already mentioned Japan. Here the state defines the areas of strategic industrial advance, initially handles the licensing, import and innovation of the relevant technologies and has, in one form or another, provided effective protection of the home market while new products are introduced. The degree to which state interaction with industry penetrates the entire economy acts as a sufficient disincentive to any conglomerate which might seek to go its own way. There are other aspects of the Japanese system which might make it a less than attractive model. But the results certainly underline the key importance of state planning and coordination in the most dynamic of the non-socialist economies. Its nearest major rival, West Germany, also relies on close relations between industrial investment and the state, and possesses a massive public sector. Energy, transport, some raw materials are all either state-run or, as in the social sector, quite heavily subsidised. The public money devoted to creating an efficient and state-planned infrastructure for industry is accepted as a necessary cost of West Germany's highly competitive and export-oriented industry. So is state expenditure on research and development which runs at 50% above the British level. In the socialist world the German Democratic Republic has overtaken British living standards within thirty years of being a war-ravaged fragment of a much larger economy. Here central state planning has been combined with a high level of local partnership with small businesses and cooperatives.

Figure 5.2

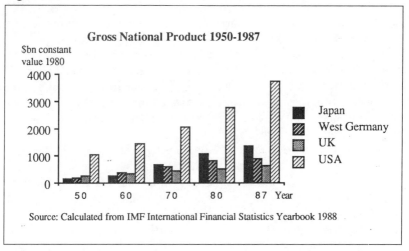

Gross National Product 1950-1987

$bn constant value 1980

Legend: Japan, West Germany, UK, USA

Years: 50, 60, 70, 80, 87 Year

Source: Calculated from IMF International Financial Statistics Yearbook 1988

There is no reason why planning — state intervention in the economy on the basis of democratically determined priorities — should have as its concomitant a closed economy. Such planning would certainly mean confronting the multinationals and limiting the right of capital to go precisely where it pleased. It would also demand a reintroduction of the restrictions, as existed up to 1979, on purely parasitic, portfolio-type capital export and this might well bring conflict with the EC. But the objective would not be that of enabling regions like Scotland to escape from the wider world. On the contrary, planned, coordinated policies of industrial development appear to be the only way of enabling such regions to survive in an international environment of the 1990s.

Planning at a Scottish level

This poses the next question. Is it possible to plan, industrially, economically, for as small a country as Scotland? Japan and West Germany both have much bigger economies than Great Britain. Scotland itself possesses less than a tenth of Britain's GDP, and has long participated in a division of labour organised at the British level. Moreover, in many sectors of production the economies of scale have now reached a pitch which demands an economic base much bigger than that of Scotland. Process plant engineering, atomic energy, aerospace, steel, chemicals and pharmaceuticals could hardly be produced competitively, for the world market, in a stand-alone Scottish economy.

In other cases, however, a combination of geography and industrial economics makes some levels of planning within Scotland realistic. These include shipbuilding and offshore engineering, whisky, structural and mechanical engineering, food processing, textiles and clothing, agriculture and fisheries, electricity generation and possibly electronics. Here either the bulk of British production is concentrated in Scotland or, as in the case of electronics, is not integrated on a British basis but internationally.

A case in point would be the offshore engineering industry. Seven-eighths of the British industry is located in Scotland — although much of it is owned by US and French multinationals and all of it, including Trafalgar House, from outside Scotland. In the fifteen years since the industry was established Scotland has become one of the three world leaders in offshore technology alongside Norway and Brazil. But as new developments in the seas around Britain slow down and exploration shifts elsewhere, the likelihood is that the multinationals will shift production and R&D facilities wherever it suits them. Given a concerted strategy with public sector involvement and accountability, and given the political will to confront and negotiate with the companies, there is no reason why this should happen. The recent disaster on the Piper Alpha platform brought home to many the immense engineering, management, and safety issues involved in offshore development. It would be a tragedy for workers in the offshore oil industry, as well as for the Scottish economy, if the immense reservoir of skills and expertise in the Scottish offshore industry were to be allowed to dissipate at the whim of a handful of multinationals. Hydrocarbon exploration worldwide will increasingly move offshore and Scotland would be well placed to become a leader in a world growth industry. But only if the correct policy steps are taken and fought for.

So in these cases strategic economic planning at Scottish level, setting investment targets, coordinating multi-firm production processes, negotiating planning agreements which allow for the transfer of technology to local and, if necessary, publicly controlled producers, is both eminently practical and economically essential. But what about the other areas of production where the scale of marketing and research and development is too large to be undertaken and planned within Scotland alone? This includes many sectors where Scotland currently has significant capacity: oil refining, gas, chemicals, pharmaceuticals — and to some extent shipbuilding and electrical and power engineering. Even offshore technology would demand a marketing strategy that is really only conceivable at British level.

It is for this reason, that of economic planning of a transregional character, that it also becomes important to look *beyond* a Scottish Parliament. A government at British level committed to planned growth would, for all the reasons of size and market power we have already noted, be a vital part of the solution for Scotland. It might also be suggested that regional assemblies elsewhere in Britain, with comparable powers to a Scottish Assembly, could have a very important role in combating the power of conglomerate capital and providing a democratic base in the regions for comprehensive planning.

One main argument of this pamphlet is that the scale of corporate power and the rapidity of takeover and divestment pose problems for all areas within Britain. Scotland has seen its own locally-controlled economy disappear in the space of thirty years. Other parts of Britain have experienced still greater relative falls in employment. Even in the south-east working people have suffered badly, in terms of housing provision and general infrastructure, from the unplanned and democratically-unaccountable concentration of economic activity in the London area. Elected assemblies, accountable to particular nations and regions, would offer the opportunity of reversing this process and taking the offensive against corporate power. It would be precisely in those areas of industrial production requiring a large-scale division of labour that such intervention would be most crucial. As we have seen, most capital in Scotland is controlled from the City of London and these conglomerate companies, dominating production in all regions, have very close links with the British state. Their typical strategy is to play one region off against another in order to gain maximum freedom for their operations. National and regional assemblies, working together, could start to reverse this process and substitute a *democratic* pressure of planning that meets the needs of their peoples.

Negotiating with big business

This brings us to the basic issue of how leverage can be applied to big business. What bargaining power can Scotland possess when faced with companies which sometimes have a turnover approaching or exceeding its own GDP?

The history of Caterpillar and many other recent closures shows what happens when a government acquiesces in the wishes of multinational companies. Is this an inevitable outcome?

It is true that a company like General Motors could virtually buy and sell the Scottish economy without noticing it. But this does not mean that national governments — or a Scottish Parliament — are unable to influence corporate decision-making. There are three principal ways in which this can, and has, been done. These are, positively, the provision of *financial and other incentives*, and, negatively, the sanctions of *market power* and the threat of *alternative production*.

Financial incentives have been used freely over the past forty years and the weaknesses of this approach are manifest. Companies can take advantage of investment grants and tax concessions and still move on once they have pocketed the cash and secured the market. At a time of high unemployment, international competitive bidding between different states and their development agencies can lead to still more damaging developments. Planning regulations, health and safety rules and employee rights can be limited in an attempt to attract companies to the most acquiescent locations. A more positive way of attracting capital is by the active development of the appropriate infrastructure and by public investment in education, training, transport and communications. This still amounts to a subsidy. But it is not one that companies can take with them if they leave. Much of the economic growth along the M4 corridor, from London to Bristol, over the past ten years can be attributed to the area's excellent infrastructure. The motorways, high-speed trains, Heathrow Airport and a chain of universities, higher education institutions and research centres guarantee the wide mix of services and highly skilled labour needed in industries like electronics and health care. A Scottish parliament with appropriate powers could ensure that similar attention is paid to Scotland's infrastructure.

At the end of the day, however, multinational firms do not just need to be offered carrots. All too often political muscle is needed to stop them inflicting actual damage. One major sanction is the powers which governments exercise over markets. In almost any industry the public sector is, directly or indirectly, a major market. In defence procurement it is the only market and many multinationals devote at least part of their resources to defence work. In other areas the government's role is more indirect but still potentially powerful.

Take, once more, the example of Caterpillar. The number of tracked vehicles bought annually by the public sector in Britain is quite small. But most of Caterpillar's earth-moving equipment is in fact used on publicly-financed projects — even though private contractors do the work. In road building, open cast mining, land reclamation and military contracting it is ultimately the government which foots the bill. Governments throughout the world use such market powers to influence corporate decision-making. Had Malcolm Rifkind wanted to stop the Caterpillar closure he could have secured a Cabinet agreement, in true Conservative style, that Caterpillar be informally given to understand that companies using their equipment would find it more difficult to get public sector contracts. More democratic governments might operate more openly.

This market power extends across a wide range of industries which are of great importance to Scotland. In computing, the goverment, the nationalised industries, the Health Service, local government and the universities together constitute a very significant part of the final market for many computer products. A company which steadfastly refused to upgrade its research, development and marketing functions within Scotland might take a different view if it knew that a Scottish parliament would make it difficult for it to sell its products to the public sector. It would be even more likely to do so if there was a British government with a similar commitment and ten times the market power.

Finally, there is the power that stems from the ability to *transfer production* if the company fails to meet obligations or threatens to close plants. The most powerful deterrent to any company is the knowledge that its products can be readily substituted. Conversely, the strongest position for a company is when, as in many third world countries, there is a complete absence of the technological or social infrastructure required for such a transfer. In those circumstances a company can dictate its own terms, including insistence that the product be imported virtually ready-made, and be confident that it can cripple the economy if it does not get its way. Clearly the size of an economy and the strength and technological sophistication of its public sector are key in such negotiations. In this context it should be remembered that Japan's economic growth was to a large extent dependent on a state-orchestrated transfer of technology from overseas to its own firms. Or, to take a different social system, the agreements currently being struck for joint production between multinational firms and the Soviet Union make provision for the progressive transfer of the technology to the host economy through planned linkages with local public enterprises.

What kind of Scottish parliament?

This brings us almost to our conclusion. We have reviewed the character of Scotland's economy. The dominant positions in virtually every industry is held by non-Scottish capital. There are virtually no big firms, competitive on the international market, which could be described as Scottish — alongside German, French or Japanese — and which repatriate capital to a Scottish base. Most of the firms which dominate the Scottish economy are owned from the City of London and protected by the British state. If we take the leverage powers which we have just examined, the Scottish economy is today, in terms of its manufacturing sector, smaller that it was ten years ago, with a much less significant public sector and has altogether lost its technological base in a number of industries.

It is against this background that we have to assess the ability of the Scottish economy to meet the challenges of 1990s and the kind of powers a Scottish parliament would need. There can be little doubt that the economic environment will be still harsher. The coming of the European Single Market will demand the removal of all remaining restriction on the movement of capital and the location of production. The drive towards concentration and still bigger conglomerates is already gathering momentum, and is likely to focus production in the central core of the Common Market. On a world scale conflicts between the different trading blocs, Japan, America and West Europe, will become considerably more intense as the new EC regulations take effect. How, then, can a Scottish parliament halt the further erosion of the country's industrial base?

One proposal is for a Scottish parliament that would be sovereign 'within

Europe'. This seeks to use the bargaining powers of an independent Scottish state within the institutions of the European Community. Superficially this might seem to have some attractions. Scotland, like Ireland or Greece, would be able to put its case directly within the European Commission. But considered against the realities of economic life it would be highly dangerous. A Scottish parliament, as things stand at the moment, would have virtually no power over those who control the country's economic resources. These are all owned from outside. *Any* attempt to apply pressure to these companies would be in violation of the European Treaty and the terms of the Single European Market.

Restrictions on the movement of capital out of Scotland, any attempt to provide special incentives to attract capital, such as the provision of grants or infrastructure, in particular any attempt to use the sanctions of power over the internal market would be ruled as incompatible with membership of the European Community. Independence in this sense, would only be formal. It would not, and could not, extend to any real powers to plan and control Scotland's economy.

There is also another factor in the exercise of power which we have so far hardly considered. This is the strength and bargaining power of organised labour. If capital is united at the level of particular states, and relies on the support and protection of its 'own' government, then the corresponding strength of any movement towards socially defined goals will inevitably depend on how far the labour movement is united and mobilised. In terms of political reality, there is no other force that potentially has sufficient coherence or common interest.

It is for this reason that the kind of Scottish parliament that is proposed here is not one that would be 'independent' and rule a separate Scotland. On the contrary, it would seek to maximise both the power of the Scottish people to control their economic and social life and at the same time, strengthen the links that exist with working people elsewhere in Britain. It would seek to ally the aspirations of the people of Scotland to control their economy — in face of unaccountable and externally controlled capital — with the similar wishes of the people elsewhere in Britain. The realities of economic power, which we have examined at length in this pamphlet, would seem to demand this. The companies which control Scotland are, in the main, owned at British level and depend on the British state. Pressure would have to be exerted at this level. It could ultimately only come from a series of regional and national alliances that are built around the organised labour movement. And, moreover, it would have to be done in the face of opposition from the Common Market. It would require a government that had the economic muscle and market power to resist and, if need be, reject, EEC regulations.

Powers a Scottish Assembly must have

Our argument is therefore for a Scottish parliament with devolved powers. We need a Scottish parliament able to take initiatives within a British framework, to plan for some areas of production, to negotiate coordinated planning perspectives for larger-scale processes and to control its own industrial and social infrastructure.

These powers would therefore include:

* strategic economic planning powers for industries, like whisky, offshore engineering, food processing, clothing and textiles, agriculture and related land uses, some areas of engineering, and possibly electronics; where the Scottish industry is not inextricably integrated in the structure of the UK industry.

* powers to coordinate the planning of the Scottish component of UK industries where scale demands UK planning; petrochemicals, power and process plant engineering, pharmaceuticals, atomic energy, aerospace and steel are amongst the most important.

* power, via revived and strengthened Scottish Development Agency/Highlands and Islands Development Board, to negotiate with multinationals over the terms of inward investment, with the object of integrating inward investment into the wider economy and ensuring where possible technology transfer which benefits the local economy.

* powers over education and training policy, vital both for the maximum development of the human potential of Scotland's people, and for the developing labour requirements of a dynamic, modern economy.

* power to restore to public ownership those parts of the Scottish public sector which have been, or are being, privatised. Most significantly, this includes electricity generation and distribution and the bus network, both of which have been accepted as being the specific responsibility of the Scottish Office and answerable to the Secretary of State for Scotland throughout the period of their public ownership.

* responsibility for industrial research and development policy with a coordinating function in this area for industries with a wider UK base.

* responsibility for monopolies and mergers policy within Scotland. This could mean the establishment of a Scottish Monopolies Commission to act as an effective watchdog over any attempted takeovers of remaining Scottish companies, or their integration into multinational operations.

* power to establish a Scottish international trading organisation initially with public finance but which, in the long term would be self-financing, to assist in the development of Scottish manufacturing exports, by providing companies with export assistance, modelled on the Japanese international trading corporations.

Financing a Scottish parliament

A Parliament with such powers would require considerable financial independence if it was to be democratically accountable, in the first instance, to the Scottish people rather than existing in a relationship of dependence on the UK Parliament. It is, however, recognised that whilst the powers proposed for the parliament are considerable, the UK Parliament will continue to be sovereign in a number of areas and, in particular, in respect of international relations and industrial planning in those sectors where economies of scale make a nonsense of a separate Scottish industry.

In order to reflect this slightly complex relationship, the Parliament should be financed from two sources:

*   a block grant from Westminster on an agreed basis as discussed in the 1979 White Paper which would reflect the greater public expenditure requirements of Scotland compared to the rest of the United Kingdom, largely because of Scotland's geography. Critics of such a proposal who think that in seeking a Scottish parliament and seeking to maintain the current Scottish proportion of UK public expenditure we are having it both ways should remember the immense contribution which the oil revenues from the Scottish sector of the North Sea have made to the Exchequer over the years.

*   a proportion of the income tax raised in Scotland, and power to vary the standard rate of income tax (up or down) in order to provide an independent and democratically accountable source of income. The precise level of the block grant and the proportion of the total Scottish income tax stake which would go to the Scottish Parliament would, of course, need to be the subject of detailed negotiation. The economic powers argued for in this pamphlet could, if quantified, provide the basis for a realistic approach to such negotiations.

Conclusion

The policy proposals in this pamphlet are not written on tablets of stone. They are, however, based on a more detailed and systematic analysis of what has been happening in the Scottish economy over the past few years than has yet been produced as the basis for proposals on constitutional change. On the evidence it is clear that Scotland's long-lived economic problems have solutions: that there are clear and realistic prospects for the future which will put our people back to work; and that these things are achievable. In order to achieve them, however, we require political change. It is hoped that the production of this pamphlet has provided helpful and specific proposals which might form the basis of such change, and in doing so help the Scottish people claim their future.

FURTHER READING

General
Tony Dickson (ed), *Scottish Capitalism,* Lawrence and Wishart, 1981
Charlotte Lythe and Madhavi Majmudar, *The Renaissance of the Scottish Economy?,* Allan and Unwin, 1982
Neil Hood and Stephen Young, *Industry, Policy and the Scottish Economy,* Edinburgh University Press, 1984
Donald Mackay (ed), *Scotland 1980: The Economics of Self-Government,* Q Press, 1977
Richard Saville, *The Economic Development of Modern Scotland,* John Donald, 1985
A. Scott, A. McKinnon and A. Reid, *Completing the Internal Market: Some Implications for the Scottish Economy,* STUC, 1988
Central Statistical Office, *Regional Trends,* (HMSO)
The following periodicals contain both relevant statistics and informed commentary: Scottish Trade Union Review (STUC), Fraser of Allander Quarterly Bulletin, Scottish Economic Bulletin (Scottish Office), Scottish Business Insider.

Ownership and control
Brian Ashcroft, James Love and James Schouller, *The Economic Effects of Inward Acquisition of Scottish Manufacturing Companies 1965–1980,* Industry Department Scotland, ESU Research Paper 11, 1987
John Firn, 'External Control and Regional Policy', in Gordon Brown (ed), *Red Paper on Scotland,* EUSPB, 1975
N. Hood, A. Reeves and S. Young, 'Foreign Direct Investment in Scotland', *Scottish Journal of Political Economy,* Vol. 28, 1981
N. Hood and S. Young, *The Multinationals in Retreat,* Edinburgh University Press, 1982
John Scott and Michael Hughes, *The Anatomy of Scottish Capital,* Croom Helm, 1980
Thorold Mackie, 'The Fall of the Scottish Quoted Firm', *Scottish Business Insider,* September, 1987
John MacInnes, 'Economic Restructuring Relevant to Industrial Relations in Scotland', *CURR Discussion Paper 26,* University of Glasgow, 1987
A.C.C. Taylor, 'Overseas Ownership in Scottish Manufacturing Industry', *Scottish Economic Bulletin,* No 33, 1986
Jordan's Top 500 Scottish Firms

Monopoly and concentration

S. Duncan, *The Local State and Uneven Development,* Polity Press, 1988
Ben Fine and Laurence Harris, *The Peculiarities of the British Economy,* Lawrence and Wishart, 1985
Laurence Harris and Jerry Coakley, *City of Capital,* Basil Blackwell, 1983
David Harvey, *The Limits to Capital,* Basil Blackwell, 1982
Richard Harris, 'Market Structure and External Control in the Regional Economies of Great Britain', *Scottish Journal of Political Economy,* Vol 35, 1988
Doreen Massey, *Spatial Divisions of Labour,* Macmillan, 1985
R. Minami, *The Economic Development of Japan,* Macmillan, 1986
K. Yamamura and Y. Yasuba, *Political Economy of Japan,* Stanford University Press, 1987
Chalmers Johnston, *MITI and the Japanese Economic Miracle,* Stanford University Press, 1981
Graham Hall (ed), *European Industrial Policy,* Croom Helm, 1986

Consequences for the Scottish economy

Brian Ashcroft, as cited above
M. Danson (ed), *Redundancies and Recession and Restructuring the Regions,* Geo Books, 1986
J. Cawdery and A.C.C. Taylor, 'Branch Plant Performance in Scotland', *Scottish Economic Bulletin,* No 32, 1985
John Foster and Charles Woolfson, *The Politics of the UCS Work-In,* Lawrence and Wishart, 1986
Bo Strath, *The Politics of De-industrialisation: the Contraction of the Western European Shipbuilding Industry,* Croom Helm, 1987
Charles Woolfson and John Foster, *Track Record: The Story of the Caterpillar Occupation,* Verso, 1988

What can be done?

Standing Commission on the Scottish Economy, *Interim Report,* 1988
Standing Commission on the Scottish Economy, *Final Report,* 1989
STUC, *Scotland: A Land Fit for People,* 1987

THE AUTHORS

Steven Boyle is an economist who has worked at the Fraser of Allender Institute at the University of Strathclyde.

Malcolm Burns is a researcher at the Trade Union Research Unit (Scotland).

Michael Danson is lecturer in economics at Paisley College.

John Foster is Professor of Applied Social Studies at Paisley College.

Douglas Harrison is Assistant Secretary (Research) at the Scottish Trades Union Congress.

Charles Woolfson is a lecturer in the Department of Social and Economic Research at the University of Glasgow.